D1761291

WISE SAYINGS

from

THE
PSALMS

LION

Compiled by Kate Kirkpatrick

A Lion Book
an imprint of
Lion Hudson plc
Wilkinson House, Jordan Hill Road,
Oxford OX2 8DR, England
www.lionhudson.com
ISBN 978 0 7459 5534 6

Distributed by:
UK: Marston Book Services, PO Box 269,
Abingdon, Oxon, OX14 4YN
USA: Trafalgar Square Publishing, 814 N.
Franklin Street, Chicago, IL 60610
USA Christian Market: Kregel Publications,
PO Box 2607, Grand Rapids, MI 49501
First edition 2011
10 9 8 7 6 5 4 3 2 1 0

Acknowledgments
pp. 10, 25, 30, 43, 46: Scripture quotations
are from the New Revised Standard Version
published by HarperCollins Publishers,
copyright © 1989 by the Division of
Christian Education of the National Council
of the Churches of Christ in the USA,
and are used by permission. All rights
reserved. pp. 12, 20, 22–23, 34, 48–49:
Scripture quotations are from The Holy
Bible, English Standard Version, published by
HarperCollins Publishers, copyright © 2001
Crossway Bibles, a division of Good News
Publishers. Used by permission. All rights
reserved. pp. 15, 26–27, 38–39, 44–45,
55, 58–59: Scripture quotations taken
from the *Holy Bible, New International Version*,
copyright © 1973, 1978, 1984 International
Bible Society. Used by permission of
Zondervan and Hodder & Stoughton
Limited. All rights reserved. The 'NIV' and
'New International Version' trademarks are
registered in the United States Patent and
Trademark Office by International Bible

Society. Use of either trademark requires
the permission of International Bible
Society. UK trademark number 1448790.
pp. 11, 24: Scripture quotations are taken
from the *Holy Bible, New Living Translation*,
copyright © 1996. Used by permission of
Tyndale House Publishers, Inc., Wheaton,
Illinois 60189. All rights reserved. Taken
from the New Jerusalem Bible, published
and copyright © 1985 by Darton, Longman
and Todd Ltd and les Editions du Cerf,
and by Doubleday, a division of Bantam
Doubleday Dell Publishing Group, Inc.
Used by permission of Darton, Longman
and Todd Ltd, and Doubleday, a division of
Random House, Inc. pp. 6, 13, 31, 52–53:
Extracts from the Authorized Version of the
Bible (The King James Bible), the rights
in which are vested in the Crown,
are reproduced by permission of the Crown's
Patentee, Cambridge University Press.
pp. 14, 16–17, 33, 36–37, 42, 54, 56–57:
Scripture quotations are from the Holy
Bible, Today's New International Version.
Copyright © 2004 by International Bible
Society. Used by permission of Hodder
& Stoughton Publishers. A member of
the Hachette Livre UK Group. All rights
reserved. 'TNIV' is a registered trademark
of International Bible Society. pp. 21, 35,
47: Scripture quotations are from New
Jerusalem Bible (NJB) From The Jerusalem
Bible © 1966 by Darton, Longman & Todd
Ltd and Doubleday & Company, Inc. Taken
from the New Jerusalem Bible, published
and copyright © 1985 by Darton, Longman
and Todd Ltd and les Editions du Cerf,
and by Doubleday, a division of Bantam
Doubleday Dell Publishing Group, Inc.
Used by permission of Darton, Longman
and Todd Ltd, and Doubleday, a division of
Random House, Inc.

A catalogue record for this book is available
from the British Library
Typeset in 10.5/12 Perpetua and 10/24
Zapfino
Printed and bound in China

CONTENTS

INTRODUCTION

Throughout the ages the Psalms have been cherished for their poetic beauty and spiritual wisdom.

This collection brings together celebrated passages from one of the best-loved books of the Bible. Exploring a wide range of human emotions – whether joy or petition, isolation or peace – these ancient meditations speak to the hearts of men and women today as insightfully as when they were first written.

The fear of the Lord is the beginning of wisdom …

Psalm 111:10

wisdom

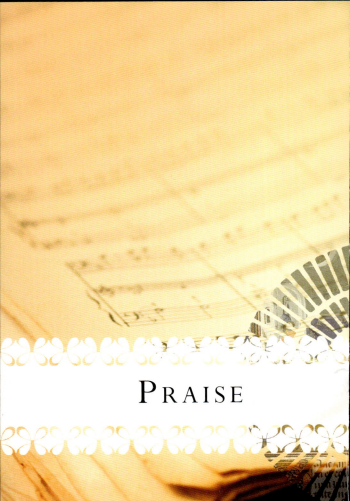

PRAISE

The heavens are telling the glory of God;
and the firmament proclaims his handiwork.
Day to day pours forth speech;
and night to night declares knowledge.
There is no speech, nor are there words;
their voice is not heard;
yet their voice goes out through all the earth,
and their words to the end of the world.

PSALM 19:1–4

I will exalt you, my God and King,
and praise your name for ever and ever.
I will praise you every day;
yes, I will praise you for ever.
Great is the Lord! He is most worthy of praise!
No one can measure his greatness.

PSALM 145:1–3

My heart is steadfast, O God!
I will sing and make melody with all my being!
Awake, O harp and lyre!
I will awake the dawn!
I will give thanks to you, O Lord, among the peoples;
I will sing praises to you among the nations.
For your steadfast love is great above the heavens;
your faithfulness reaches to the clouds.

Be exalted, O God,
above the heavens!
Let your glory be over all the
earth!

PSALM 108:1–5

Bless the Lord, O my soul: and all that is
within me, bless his holy name.
Bless the Lord, O my soul, and forget
not all his benefits:
Who forgiveth all thine iniquities;
who healeth all thy diseases;
Who redeemeth thy life from destruction;
who crowneth thee with loving kindness
and tender mercies;
Who satisfieth thy mouth with good
things; so that thy youth is renewed like
the eagle's.

PSALM 103:1–5

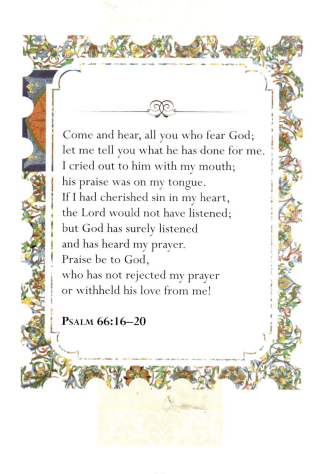

Come and hear, all you who fear God;
let me tell you what he has done for me.
I cried out to him with my mouth;
his praise was on my tongue.
If I had cherished sin in my heart,
the Lord would not have listened;
but God has surely listened
and has heard my prayer.
Praise be to God,
who has not rejected my prayer
or withheld his love from me!

PSALM 66:16–20

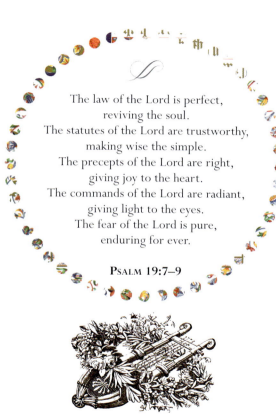

The law of the Lord is perfect,
reviving the soul.
The statutes of the Lord are trustworthy,
making wise the simple.
The precepts of the Lord are right,
giving joy to the heart.
The commands of the Lord are radiant,
giving light to the eyes.
The fear of the Lord is pure,
enduring for ever.

PSALM 19:7–9

When I consider your heavens,
the work of your fingers,
the moon and the stars,
which you have set in place,
what are mere mortals that you are mindful of them,
human beings that you care for them?
You have made them a little lower than the heavenly beings
and crowned them with glory and honour.

glory and honour

You made them rulers over the works of your hands;
you put everything under their feet:
all flocks and herds,
and the animals of the wild,
the birds in the sky,
and the fish in the sea,
all that swim the paths of the seas.

Lord, our Lord,
how majestic is your name
in all the earth!

PSALM 8:3–9

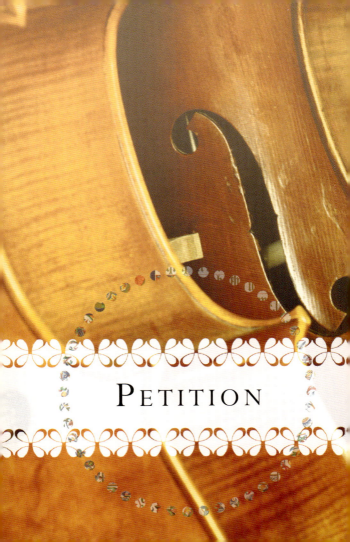

PETITION

My God, my God, why have you forsaken me?
Why are you so far from saving me,
from the words of my groaning?
O my God, I cry by day, but you do not answer,
and by night, but I find no rest.
Yet you are holy,
enthroned on the praises of Israel.
In you our fathers trusted;
they trusted, and you delivered them.
To you they cried and were rescued;
in you they trusted and were not put to shame.

PSALM 22:1–5

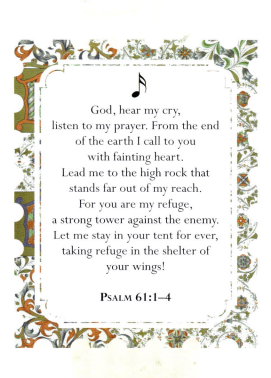

God, hear my cry,
listen to my prayer. From the end
of the earth I call to you
with fainting heart.
Lead me to the high rock that
stands far out of my reach.
For you are my refuge,
a strong tower against the enemy.
Let me stay in your tent for ever,
taking refuge in the shelter of
your wings!

PSALM 61:1–4

Save me, O God!
For the waters have come up to my neck.
I sink in deep mire,
where there is no foothold;
I have come into deep waters,
and the flood sweeps over me.
I am weary with my crying out;
my throat is parched.
My eyes grow dim
with waiting for my God.

More in number than the hairs of my head
are those who hate me without cause;
mighty are those who would destroy me,
those who attack me with lies.
What I did not steal
must I now restore?
O God, you know my folly;
the wrongs I have done are not hidden from you.

For zeal for your house has consumed me,
and the reproaches of those who reproach you
have fallen on me.
When I wept and humbled my soul with fasting,
it became my reproach.
When I made sackcloth my clothing,
I became a byword to them.
I am the talk of those who sit in the gate,
and the drunkards make songs about me.

But as for me, my prayer is to you, O Lord.
At an acceptable time, O God,
in the abundance of your steadfast love answer me
in your saving faithfulness.
Deliver me from sinking in the mire;
let me be delivered from my enemies
and from the deep waters.
Let not the flood sweep over me,
or the deep swallow me up,
or the pit close its mouth over me.

Answer me, O Lord,
for your steadfast love is good;
according to your abundant mercy,
turn to me.

PSALM 69:1–5, 9–16

Do not turn your back
on me.
Do not reject your
servant in anger.
You have always been
my helper.
Don't leave me now;
don't abandon me,
O God of my salvation!

PSALM 27:9

Save me, O God, by your name,
and vindicate me by your might.
Hear my prayer, O God;
give ear to the words of my mouth.
For the insolent have risen against me,
the ruthless seek my life;
they do not set God before them.
Selah
But surely, God is my helper;
the Lord is the upholder of my life.

PSALM 54:1–4

As the deer pants for streams of water,
so my soul pants for you, O God.
My soul thirsts for God, for the living God.
When can I go and meet with God?
My tears have been my food day and night,
while people say to me all day long,
"Where is your God?"
These things I remember
as I pour out my soul:
how I used to go with the multitude,
leading the procession to the house of God,
with shouts of joy and thanksgiving
among the festive throng.

Why are you downcast,
O my soul?
Why so disturbed within me?
Put your hope in God,
for I will yet praise him,
my Saviour and my God.

PSALM 42:1–6

thirsts

PEACE

The heavens are yours, the earth also is yours;
the world and all that is in it – you have founded them.
The north and the south – you created them;
Tabor and Hermon joyously praise your name.
You have a mighty arm;
strong is your hand, high your right hand.
Righteousness and justice are the foundation of
your throne;
steadfast love and faithfulness go before you.
Happy are the people who know the festal shout,
who walk, O Lord, in the light of your countenance;
they exult in your name all day long,
and extol your righteousness.
For you are the glory of their strength;
by your favour our horn is exalted.

PSALM 89:11–17

Be still, and know that

I am God.

Psalm 46:10

O Lord, my heart is not lifted up;
My eyes are not raised too high
for thee;
I do not think on things too great
or marvellous;
Or matters too difficult for me.
But I have calmed and quieted
my soul;
Like a weaned child with its mother;
Like a weaned child is my soul
within me.
O Israel, trust in the Lord
From this time forth and forevermore.

ADAPTED FROM PSALM 131

How good and pleasant it is
when God's people live together in unity!
It is like precious oil poured on the head,
running down on the beard,
running down on Aaron's beard,
down on the collar of his robe.
It is as if the dew of Hermon
were falling on Mount Zion.
For there the Lord bestows his blessing,
even life forevermore.

PSALM 133

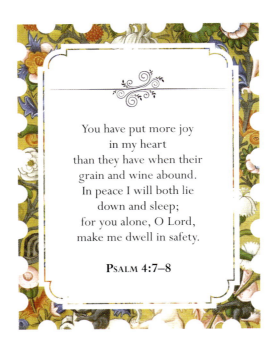

You have put more joy
in my heart
than they have when their
grain and wine abound.
In peace I will both lie
down and sleep;
for you alone, O Lord,
make me dwell in safety.

PSALM 4:7–8

When I am afraid,
I put my trust in you,
in God, whose word I praise,
in God I put my trust and
have no fear.

PSALM 56:3–4

You have searched me, Lord,
and you know me.

You know when I sit and when I rise;
you perceive my thoughts from afar.

You discern my going out and my lying down;
you are familiar with all my ways.

Before a word is on my tongue
you, Lord, know it completely.

You hem me in behind and before,
and you lay your hand upon me.

Such knowledge is too wonderful for me,
too lofty for me to attain.

Where can I go from your Spirit?
Where can I flee from your presence?

If I go up to the heavens, you are there;
if I make my bed in the depths, you are there.

If I rise on the wings of the dawn,
if I settle on the far side of the sea,

even there your hand will guide me,
your right hand will hold me fast.

If I say, "Surely the darkness will hide me
and the light become night around me,"

even the darkness will not be dark to you;
the night will shine like the day,
for darkness is as light to you.

For you created my inmost being;
you knit me together in my mother's womb.

I praise you because I am fearfully and
wonderfully made;
your works are wonderful,

I know that full well.

PSALM 139:1–14

How lovely is your dwelling-place,
O Lord Almighty!
My soul yearns, even faints,
for the courts of the Lord;
my heart and my flesh cry out
for the living God.

Better is one day in your courts
than a thousand elsewhere;
I would rather be a doorkeeper
in the house of my God
than dwell in the tents of the wicked.

For the Lord God is a sun and shield;
the Lord bestows favour and honour;
no good thing does he withhold
from those whose walk is blameless.

O Lord Almighty,
blessed are those who trust in you.

PSALM 84:1–2, 10–12

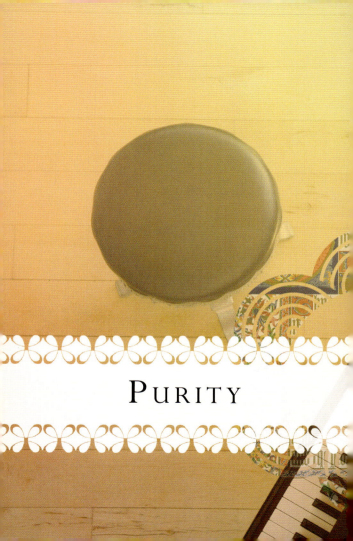

PURITY

Create in me
a pure heart,
O God.

PSALM 51:10

The Lord is merciful and gracious,
slow to anger and abounding in steadfast love.

He will not always accuse,
nor will he keep his anger for ever.

He does not deal with us according to our sins,
nor repay us according to our iniquities.

For as the heavens are high above the earth,
so great is his steadfast love toward those who fear him;

as far as the east is from the west,
so far he removes our transgressions from us.

PSALM 103:8–12

How can the young keep their
way pure?
By living according to your word.

I seek you with all my heart;
do not let me stray from your commands.

I have hidden your word in my heart
that I might not sin against you.

Praise be to you, O Lord;
teach me your decrees.

With my lips I recount all the laws
that come from your mouth.

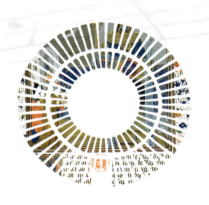

I rejoice in following your statutes
as one rejoices in great riches.

I meditate on your precepts
and consider your ways.

I delight in your decrees;
I will not neglect your word.

PSALM 119:9–16

O Lord, who may abide in your tent?
Who may dwell on your holy hill?

Those who walk blamelessly, and do what is right,
and speak the truth from their heart;
who do not slander with their tongue,
and do no evil to their friends,
nor take up a reproach against their neighbours;
in whose eyes the wicked are despised,
but who honour those who fear the Lord;
who stand by their oath even to their hurt;
who do not lend money at interest,
and do not take a bribe against the innocent.
Those who do these things shall never be moved.

PSALM 15

To Yahweh belong the earth and all it contains,
the world and all who live there;
it is he who laid its foundations on the seas,
on the flowing waters fixed it firm.

Who shall go up to the mountain of Yahweh?
Who shall take a stand in his holy place?

The clean of hands and pure of heart,
whose heart is not set on vanities,
who does not swear an oath in order to deceive.

Such a one will receive blessing from Yahweh,
saving justice from the God of his salvation.

PSALM 24:1–5

Behold, you delight in truth in the inward being,
and you teach me wisdom in the secret heart.

Purge me with hyssop, and I shall be clean;
wash me, and I shall be whiter than snow.
Let me hear joy and gladness;
let the bones that you have broken rejoice.
Hide your face from my sins,
and blot out all my iniquities.
Create in me a clean heart, O God,
and renew a right spirit within me.
Cast me not away from your presence,
and take not your Holy Spirit from me.

Restore to me the joy of
your salvation,
and uphold me with a
willing spirit.

PSALM 51:6–12

willing spirit

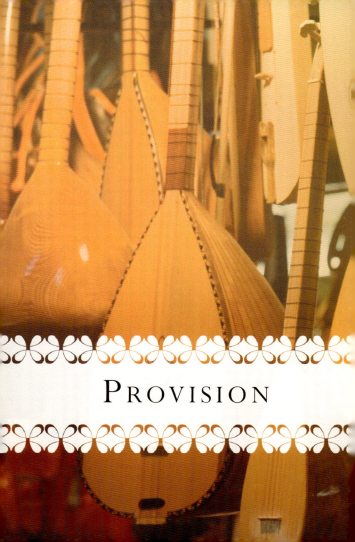

PROVISION

The Lord is my shepherd; I shall not want.

He maketh me to lie down in green pastures:
he leadeth me beside the still waters.

He restoreth my soul: he leadeth me in the paths
of righteousness for his name's sake.

Yea, though I walk through the valley of the
shadow of death, I will fear no evil:
for thou art with me;
thy rod and thy staff they comfort me.

Thou preparest a table before me in the presence
of mine enemies: thou anointest my head with oil;
my cup runneth over.

Surely goodness and mercy shall follow me all the days of my life: and I will dwell in the house of the Lord for ever.

PSALM 23

Blessed are those
who do not walk in step with the wicked
or stand in the way that sinners take
or sit in the company of mockers,

but who delight in the law of the Lord,
and meditate on his law day and night.

They are like a tree planted by streams of water,
which yields its fruit in season
and whose leaf does not wither –
whatever they do prospers.

PSALM 1:1–3

Do not fret because of those who are evil or be envious of those who do wrong; for like the grass they will soon wither, like green plants they will soon die away.

Trust in the Lord and do good; dwell in the land and enjoy safe pasture.Delight yourself in the Lord and he will give you the desires of your heart.

Commit your way to the Lord; trust in him and he will do this: He will make your righteousness shine like the dawn, the justice of your cause like the noonday sun.

Psalm 37:1–6

Whoever dwells in the shelter of the Most High
will rest in the shadow of the Almighty.
They say of the Lord, "He is my refuge and my
fortress, my God, in whom I trust."

Surely he will save you
from the fowler's snare
and from the deadly pestilence.
He will cover you with his feathers,
and under his wings you will find refuge;
his faithfulness will be your shield and rampart.
You will not fear the terror of night,
nor the arrow that flies by day,
nor the pestilence that stalks in the darkness,
nor the plague that destroys at midday.
A thousand may fall at your side,
ten thousand at your right hand,
but it will not come near you.
You will only observe with your eyes
and see the punishment of the wicked.

If you say, "The Lord is my refuge,"
and you make the Most High your dwelling,
no harm will overtake you,
no disaster will come near your tent.
For he will command his angels concerning you
to guard you in all your ways;
they will lift you up in their hands,
so that you will not strike your foot against a stone.
You will tread on the lion and the cobra;
you will trample the great lion and the serpent.

"Because they love me," says the Lord,
"I will rescue them; I will protect them,
for they acknowledge my name.
They will call on me, and I will answer them;
I will be with them in trouble,
I will deliver them and honour them.
With long life I will satisfy them
and show them my salvation."

PSALM 91

I lift up my eyes to the hills —
where does my help come from?

My help comes from the Lord,
the Maker of heaven and earth.

He will not let your foot slip —
he who watches over you will not slumber;

your shade

indeed, he who watches over Israel
will neither slumber nor sleep.

The Lord watches over you –
the Lord is your shade at your right hand;
the sun will not harm you by day,
nor the moon by night.

The Lord will keep you from all harm –
he will watch over your life;
the Lord will watch over your coming and going
both now and for evermore.

PSALM 121

ACKNOWLEDGMENTS

BACKGROUNDS:
iStock: Jussi Santaniemi

ILLUMINATED MANUSCRIPTS:
Alamy: Classic Image
Corbis: Fine Art Photographic Library; The Gallery Collection

MOTIFS:
Corbis: Bob Jacobson
iStock: Floortje; Jamie Farrant; Nicoolay; Oleksii Popovskyi

PHOTOGRAPHS:
Corbis: pp. 6–7 Ali Meyer; pp. 18–19 Bertrand Rieger/Hemis; pp. 22–23 Karl Buicker; pp. 26–27 Michael Claxton/Lebrecht Music & Arts; p. 36 Monalyn Gracia; pp. 40–41 Roger Brooks/ Beateworks; p. 49 P. Manner; pp. 50–51 David Sutherland; pp. 52–53 Michael Kai; pp. 58–59 Roy McMahon
iStock: pp. 8–9 Esolla; pp. 16–17 Eric Hood; pp. 28–29 vhsrt-just; p. 32 Peter Nguyen; pp. 38–39 Dan Van Oss; pp. 44–45 Steve Smith; p. 57 Mats Tooming

COVER
Background: Jussi Santoniemi/iStock
Illuminated manuscript: The Gallery Collection/Corbis
Photograph: Mats Tooming/iStock